Life as an Addict

The Twelve Steps that Saved My Life

by Michael Elliott

Dorrance Publishing Co
585 Alpha Drive
Suite 103
Pittsburgh, PA 15238
Visit our website at *www.dorrancebookstore.com*

ISBN: 979-8-8860-4440-9
eISBN: 979-8-8868-3861-9

Life as an Addict
The Twelve Steps that Saved My Life

This book is dedicated to the memory of my son Jonathan Michael Elliott (1999-2006), to all the people who supported me during the tough times, to my mother Betty who never gave up on me from day one, to my best friend David, and to Laurie Chilcott from the Neighborhood Center of West Volusia.

PROLOGUE
Life as an Addict

As a young man, life was going the way it should for me. I was finishing my life-long dream by finishing my last year of nursing school. All I dreamed about was helping someone's life get better, and that changed because of turmoil and pain. My life was going to be great, or so I thought. It was going to be great until that one day my life turned upside down. I was a person of such knowledge and a heart of gold challenged with decisions that I would not wish on anyone, not even my worst enemy. Choosing life and death situations for other people did not seem to be so bad, and I was faced with an ultimate fear which you will find out about later on. That was the day in my life that I became an addict. The day that changed me forever. This book is to show how I am an addict who overcame it, and I continue to fight the everyday battle of sobriety.

According to the American Addiction Center, statistics show that 8.5 million people suffer from addiction and mental health disorders, and that is only included people who are challenged with the illnesses. It does not account for the people who live life with an addiction and never seek help from a professional or never thought they were an addict because they were good at hiding their illness. Nonetheless, this illness is so misunderstood and mistreated by so many. Hopefully, with this book, I can help people understand the life of an addict and show people that suffer from this illness that they are not alone.

This is my story, and these are my great life challenges I faced as an addict. It will describe situations and experiences I endured that made me an addict and what I continue to do now to keep my sobriety. This is a lifelong process and will be with me the rest of my life.

INTRODUCTION

You might ask, what is an addiction? Simple to answer, you might think, but let me tell you, from my perspective what addiction means to me. Addiction is a way of life where you are physically, emotionally, and mentally dependent on a substance. Whether your substance is alcohol, drugs, emotions, actions, or even thinking can be a substance of addiction. This substance has been introduced into one's life and is now in control of everything you do. Your life has become unmanageable, down to the task of even taking care of yourself and your loved ones. This illness is so silent that you don't know it's knocking on your door until it's too late.

Addiction is an illness that has no prejudice on race, color, wealth, poverty, short, tall, skinny, or overweight. No matter what the classification you live by, this illness will come into your life and destroy everything you worked hard for. Your loved ones will give up and move forward with their lives, for they may have waited long enough and are tired of your excuses of not moving forward and bettering your life. It will destroy marriages, relationships, and, yes, even your own perception of yourself. Your identity will be lost from this illness, and it wants nothing more than to be the ruler of your life.

We don't choose to be an addict. Addiction chooses us from choices that we made. I made a choice when I was twenty-six years old to do my first line of cocaine which numbed me from my emotions because I suffered a tragic loss. On August 11, 2006, I had to say good-bye to my child, and he was only seven years old.

Jonathan was my first-born child and was born with a debilitating muscle disease that was unknown at the time. Jonathan lived a short life of happiness and love. Jonathan was such an inspiration to me. He drove me to be a better man. His smile would have penetrated your soul if you would have met him. Jonathan walked into the hospital one day feeling sick and just not himself. Things happened so fast that even as a nurse, I did not see what was going on. Denial may have been a part of that since it was my child. My mind told me that he was okay, and he will get through this just as he did before.

I was sitting with him alone and he was resting peacefully, and something just made me look over and check on him. The alarms started to sound off, his little heart began to slow down, and his brown eyes closed. Jonathan went into full cardiac arrest and was in my arms. I was screaming for help and no one was around to help. Feeling helpless and lost, I began chest compressions and finally the code team arrived and relieved me from saving my child's life. Jonathan was brought back but his condition was critical, and the doctors did not have any good outcomes for his condition. Jonathan lost his heart rhythm for the third time and was down too long and there was no hope. The doctors brought us all together and told us that Jonathan is clinically braindead and he suffered cardiogenic shock, which meant that all of his organs were failing to respond to any treatment.

My little boy, my baby. I cried just as I made that final decision to let Jonathan go, and on August 11, 2006, at 8:15 P.M. the advance life support that was keeping him alive and breathing was turned off. He took his last breath with his hand in my hand and the family at his side as we all said goodbye, and we love you Jon-boy. This was the day my addiction began.

Jonathan was laid to rest two days later in our hometown of Litchfield, Ohio right next to his great grandmother, who was his best buddy during the time she was alive.

The death of my son was the breaking point of my mental stability. I could not stop thinking why couldn't I have saved Jonathan if I would have just reacted sooner? I was a great nurse. Why did I not see what was right in front of me? The questions kept coming Why? Why? Why?

Then I asked GOD, why did you do this? My faith began to dwindle. Why would a GOD take such an angel from me? There was no answer I could give myself to help lift this overwhelming guilt and depression I fell into. I just wanted to feel normal again and not feel this void, this pain, and this suffering anymore.

My friend and I were out at the bar that night and I knew he was getting high and having a great time. I wanted to feel no pain, no worries, no guilt, and my thoughts were that this would be just one time. Just this one time let me escape this awful world I was living in. That is all it took was just that one time and my life began to spiral out of control. It took some time, but seven and half years later when I was arrested and sent to prison for drugs is when I realized that my life was over, and I was addicted to drugs.

My house, my cars, my money were all gone. Everything I worked hard to get was all gone. The only thing left was the little glass pipe and that bag of crystal meth laying in my lap. There was nothing more in life than that feeling I got when I used that needle to inject that substance in my vein. The pain and suffering were gone, so I thought. My emotions were just suppressed and bottled deep inside. Every time I got sober, those emotions and feelings resurfaced, and the cycle would begin again.

How far would I go before rock bottom would hit? When was enough was enough? Maybe after three arrests and the loss of quality time with friends and family was enough. Relationship after relationship came and gone. I was utterly alone going through this pain and suffering. Everybody that cared was no longer there for me. I pushed them away and they could do no more for me.

That was the day I finally said enough is enough. If I want to live to see the next day, I must get help and fight this illness with everything I had left in me. I sought help with therapy, which was wonderful. My first therapist was great. Her name was Jennie and my first time meeting her I thought she was as crazy as I was, but she was able to reach me, and she helped me in so many ways. This was my first try of being sober.

My sobriety lasted for about four years, and I thought I had control of me again, yet the loss of a job sent me spiraling out of control again and I relapsed. Again, I had to pick myself up from the bottom pit and reach once again for help, and I fell again with another relapse.

What can I do to get through this? My body can't handle much more of this abuse I was bestowing upon myself. I had scars from head to toe from IV administration. It got so bad that people began to look at me and turn away for they thought I was contagious, or they did not want to be seen with me. I looked like a man on his last leg before death. I probably was on that last leg.

Finally, one day, I began to work the twelve steps I learned from rehab and group therapy. Some liked AA, some liked NA, and others liked just group therapy. It does not matter which one you attend; it's about the people who show up and give their testimony.

While I was giving my testimony, emotions and tears fell from my face uncontrollably and this stranger extended their hand and told me, "You're not alone." "We got you," they repeated time after time. From that day, I began my journey once again, but this time I tried something different. I followed these twelve steps. These twelve steps saved my LIFE!

CHAPTER ONE
Acceptance

*Admit that we are powerless over our addiction and that
our lives had become unmanageable.*

My first twenty-six years of life, I was anti-drug use and only drank on social occasion, which was rare. I never thought I would be the one to say, "I am an addict." I remember that day I first used very distinctly. I told my friends it won't hurt me. I am only going to use it just this one time and move on.

My pain and suffering disappeared; it was just easier to just use and feel that despair and pain lift right off my shoulders than to seek help from a professional. I was never thinking that I had a problem. It went from just that one time of using to using every other weekend. Still, I had no problem with drugs, but I still was crying every day, feeling that pain and that void that nothing could fill, but just one more injection and this will all go away.

I was a person who loved to work and hardly ever missed a day of work. I got called into the office one day to talk about recent absence that occurred and all I could do was say was I was sorry and that I was under the weather. The truth be told, I just was recovering from a hard weekend of partying and no sleep. I could not tell you how many days I had been up. I was using every weekend now, but I still denied that I had a problem.

Finally, the time came, and I was asked to resign from my dream position of being a Clinical Leader at the local hospital. I loved being a Clinical Leader. I was teaching new nurses, overseeing the clinical nurses on my floor, and most of all, I was helping others get better. It was a challenging job and that was why I loved it. There was not a dull moment ever. Boredom was my enemy. I kept thinking, what I will do with my time now? Well, I am sure you can guess what my answer was to that. Let's use more drugs and this will pass, and I won't be so bored anymore and my pain and suffering will go away.

I did not look for reemployment. I just thought some time off from working would help me deal with my issues I had going on. Let's just have some fun times with my drug friends and party for a little while and not think about the problems I was having now. The bank account dwindled faster and faster each day until there was no money left. I began to panic, feeling that loss of not having my drug that would make me feel happy and my dreamscape where no problems existed. I asked myself, what should I do?

Well, let's just say it was not the best decision I could have made. My mind was so clouded with drugs that even the most rational thing to do was not rational anymore. All I thought about was when can I get more Meth, or where is the next place to party? It was never about getting another job or seeking help for my problems, for I believed I did not have any drug problems. I am in control of me, and no drug will control me. That's what I believed and kept telling myself.

It was not until I was arrested and put behind bars that I started to realize I was beginning to break down. How did I get this far? How did I let myself get this deep in my addiction? I reached out to my family and the shock came out. "What happened to you, Michael?" my mother asked. All I could say was that I have some problems that I have to work through, never leading that the problem was my drug use and my addiction has now taken control of my ability to manage my life.

It was not till I was sober for a few weeks sitting in a jail cell that I finally realized that I have become an addict and my life was unmanageable. My first step to my sobriety was accepting that I was an addict and that my life has become unmanageable. No more denial, no more excuses, no more lying to myself. I have become what I said I never would be: a drug addict. Standing up in my first group and introducing myself was the hardest thing I had to do. "Hi, my name is Michael, and I am an addict."

CHAPTER TWO
Hope

Came to believe that a power greater than ourselves could restore us to sanity.

The frustration and turmoil of being sober was not easy. Every emotion was hard to bear and face each day. All I could do was lay in my room and be angry at myself. No matter who tried to help, I just pushed them away. I lost my son, lost my life, lost my ability to live on my own. I was homeless, carless, with no money to even buy me a pack of cigarettes. How low can one get?

My sanity was at stake. I really thought I was going crazy and having a nervous breakdown. Let me just get high and that will take it away. These thoughts kept urging me and everywhere I went reminded me of my addiction and tempted me to use. When I was in the grocery store shopping and passed the candy aisle, I would have an urge to use. When I was driving my car and passed through a city I stayed in while I was getting high would give me urge to use.

Oh my GOD, what can I do? This is driving me crazy. No matter what I did I was having those urges it seemed like all day.

Every minute passed just like the ticking clock on the wall. Tick Tok Tick Tok, counting every second of every minute. Will this pain and the urge to use ever go away? My sobriety was challenged every day. Not a day goes by that I didn't think of using meth to take away my pain and suffering.

The day came when I had to the face the consequences of my decisions which had led up to my arrest. Attorney fees were outrageous, and my attorney took advantage of us because of the situation I was in. I had never been in trouble before, not even a traffic ticket. My attorney and I had a talk over the phone. I was offered a plea deal by the District Attorney. My attorney of course downplayed it and made it sound like I was only going to do a year in prison. Of course, that was not the case when I appeared in front of the judge to plead out and the sentence was read, "Ten-year sentence with five years in confinement."

My knees began to knock, all I could do was look over at my attorney and think, "You lied to me, you son of bitch, you said I would only get one year." He replied to me, saying, "The prison system is overpopulated and with your sentence, as long as you have good behavior, you will only have to do one year in prison. The rest of your time will be parole and probation." That is not what we discussed. It was too late at this point; it was done. I was taken away and sent to prison.

As I was walking up, there was a gate encased with barbed wire that looked like it went on forever. I stepped forward into the path of the closing gate which finally latched behind me. I was thinking to myself that this is a place people would never leave, and I was scared to death. I have never been in such a situation before and all I can remember is what people would say about prison life and how terrible it is.

Literally, I have never been treated so poorly as a human being. I was called so many different names, the one that was the worst was, "You're nothing but scum of the earth, you criminal." I had to endure this treatment over and over and it began to break me down even more. When I thought I was at the lowest point of my life, they would find a way to bring me down one more step.

Our judicial system was supposed to be a corrective system and help rehabilitate us so we can come back into society. To me, that was not the case. It was the worst experience I have had to endure. There was no escape from it. Mentally, I was torn apart from what little threadswere left that held me together.

Here I sat in my cell, looking at the walls and thinking about what I did to deserve this. I looked up at the ceiling and asked GOD, why me? Why did you take my son from me? Why did you put me here in such a place of madness? Why? Why?

At this point of my life, I was so vulnerable. I fell to my knees with tears swelling from each eye. "GOD, I hope you hear me now more than any other time I have prayed, please give me the hope and strength to get through this. I am weak and need your strength to return me to who I was before all this started."

Every day I woke up and the next day had come. I was taking it one day at a time. All I could do is look up and pray for strength and hope that GOD heard me. All I could do was hope that one day GOD will return me home and give me my sanity back.

With hope and faith, I was able to get through each day until finally GOD answered my prayer. I was going home. I was scared now. I had to face the world again, still having those urges to use. I looked up and said, "I hope you can help me GOD. Return my sanity so I can get home without using drugs, so I don't have to return to this awful place."

CHAPTER THREE
Willingness

Decided to turn our will and our lives over to the care of GOD as we understood him

Just when I thought that everything bad has happened and good things will finally come to me, I was wrong. I believed that it was time for me to start living my life again. I was struck with an illness. All I can say is that I thought I was going to die.

The migraines I had every day were unbearable. The body aches and the weakness overcame me. I kept asking, what is going on with me? I am eating healthy. If you know how mom's cooking was, you did not have to worry about being healthy. Everyone loved the southern soul food she cooked. Even the neighbor would come over and enjoy my mother's cooking. For some reason, it was not enough to get me better and the weight dropped of me. Not that I could afford to lose anymore pounds. I was already down to 165 pounds from 220 pounds.

After about two weeks of feeling down and no desire to do anything, I finally went to the doctor. The doctor walked in and asked, "What seems to be the problem?" My response was, "Everything, doctor." Little did I know I had a raging mouth infection going on besides what else was festering in my body. Blood work was done to see what was going on.

I was patiently waiting and not knowing what was going on. I was treated for thrush of the mouth and bacterial infection of the skin. Those problems were all finally getting better after treatment with antibiotics and antifungal pills. When the doctor came in the door to reveal my lab work results, you know when something is wrong just the way the doctor walks in the room. No eye contact, quick to sit down at his chair, and pen waving around in his hand like a cheerleader does with batons at a high school football game.

"I wish I had better news, Michael," the doctor said as he looked up at me, seeing that my face was full of fear and distraught. "Michael, you tested positive for HIV, and your T-cell count was very low."

I went home that evening and pretty much lost it. What else can go wrong, is this going to be the final kicker for me? I was challenged yet again in my life with another battle that I thought I was going to lose. Urges and temptation were so high. My image of myself was down. I kept thinking, who will love someone like m?. A drug addict, a criminal, and now I am a person living with HIV. Who will love someone like me?

Again, feeling like there was no hope, I went to group and shared my testimony. I questioned my faith, I questioned my judgement, literally, I questioned everything about my life and existence. Why am I here? All I have is pain and suffering. The only thing I knew that took the pain away was using a substance to numb me and help me forget what I was going through.

Just as I was telling my testimony again, there was that hand that extended to me yet again and told me, "It will be okay; we got you. You're not alone in this. All you got to do is open your arms and let GOD take it from here" So that is what I did. I looked up and said to myself, "GOD, if you are listening to me, please help me. GOD, please with your almighty power help me get through this."

Willingness to let my higher being come into my life was hard to do after everything I had been through. As a child, it was easy to understand, but as an adult, my faith in GOD was weakened. It was time to gain that faith I once had. I understood that it was not going to be easy but with him by my side, I had the urge to continue. The weight was lifted off my shoulders as I opened my heart and soul to him and understood now what he meant to me in my life.

CHAPTER FOUR
Personal Inventory

Made a searching and fearless moral inventory of ourselves.

Life is like a deck of cards. What you're dealt is what you must live with. Depending on how you look at this, it can be a great hand like a Royal Flush, or you could have been dealt a bust hand with a nine of hearts and two of spades. I looked at my life and wondered what kind of hand I was dealt. I'll leave that up to you to decide.

My family, especially my mother, has had my back through this journey. I look back now and see the pain I caused her emotionally, physically, and financially. My mother took her retirement to get me out of jail and paid for my attorney fees. Let's just say, your family is all you have that will be there for you. No one else would have done what they did for me to help me during my days of failure and triumph. Once they found out about my drug use and my ways of living, there was a tremendous strain on our relationship.

"How many times will I have to do this?" my mother said to me. "You were a golden child but what happened to you? Where did we go wrong?" I realized that my actions not only affected me, but they also affected everyone around me that cared.

I have a great education. In total, I have been in college five times with different types of degrees ranging from medical to business. I have always loved to learn and that is the perfectionist side of me. I have a lot to offer someone, whether it be a working relationship or a romantic relationship. My heart is like gold, but with all this turmoil, my way of feeling had changed.

The death of my son has given me strength to deal with heartache and strength to deal with stressful situations and emotions. I see that now with my sobriety, but during my drug use, I found that it was also my weakness. I used my situations to further my depression. I wanted someone else to feel what I was feeling. I know I am not the only person who has lost a child but having a void in my life was the deepest, darkest side of my life. That was not who I was or who I wanted to be. I wanted to be happy and feel whole again.

During this journey of drug use, I met some great people that had not admitted yet they were addicts, but I hope their day will come just like mine. I grieve the loss of my friends for I know that my temptations grew stronger around them and they were still using, and I could not put myself in that situation if I am going to stay sober unless they were sober themselves. Even then, it was still hard on me to be around them and not have that craving. It was a reminder of what great times we had together.

Ironically, yes, the times I had with my friends were not bad ones. There was always a good conversation that would last for hours. There was great sex with those individuals that advanced with intimacy. I had to let go of these memories and move forward and know that the time I had with them was short-lived but good, but it could no longer be.

I was thinking hopefully that they will understand why I had to say goodbye, and what we had once will no longer be. My life and health were more important than to continue with such a lifestyle. It will be hard, but with my experience, I will get through this just like I did before.

The fear of making new friends and relationships is real. It's hard to think at my age what will I do to make new friends and where would I find people to befriend. I am still experimenting with this. I am trying new places, new things, and new people cautiously for I know what my weaknesses are now, and I can't slip into something that will challenge my sobriety.

CHAPTER FIVE
Self-Disclosure

Admitted to GOD, to ourselves, and to another human being the exact nature of our wrongs.

One of the hardest things I had to endure was watching my daughter go through this pain and suffering. My drug use not only took precious time from her, but it also took moments that I will not be able to experience ever again. My little girl went from piggy tails and holding on to me for safety and security to a grown-up lady overnight it seemed.

I asked myself, where has my little girl gone? Then, I looked back at those times I was missing or gone from her life from my drug use. I never used around my daughter nor did I want her to see me that way, so I always took myself out of the situation. The pain and emotional strain I felt when my mother would tell me that my daughter was looking for me. "Where's my daddy? Where did he go?" I was off on a binge somewhere getting high. There were times when she was crying and needed her father to protect her from the smallest things like the closet monster that kept her from sleeping at night to those things your daughter comes to her father when she does not understand. This is time, I will never get back.

I think to myself now being sober what damage have I done to our relationship? Will it be repairable, or better yet, will she ever forgive me for what I have done to her? The choice of drugs should never be before your child, GOD, what was I thinking? I have already lost one child, and here I am using drugs from one loss and because of my choices, I may end up losing my other child if I don't change my ways.

"GOD, please forgive me for my wrong doings to my daughter and my family. You are the only one who knows why I have done what I've done. There is no excuse for my actions towards my precious little girl. GOD, I have an illness with an addiction, and I have lost my way."

After a few months into my sobriety, I finally had the courage to face my daughter. In the car, on our way to the store, I grabbed her hand and looked in her in the eyes and said, "Honey, you know daddy loves you." Tears swelled in her eyes. It took everything I had not to break down in front of her and cry.

"You know daddy has been sick. I have an illness called addiction. This illness has taken so much from you, and it's not your fault," I stressed dramatically to her. "I am sorry for not being the father I should have been, but if you give me that chance, I will make sure it never happens again."

There is no other feeling in the world than that unconditional love you get from your child. It's something I don't want to lose. I will make that change not only for myself but for her. She deserves a father that will be there no matter what, and I promise I will do my best to fight this illness we call addiction so I can be with her for what time we have left.

CHAPTER SIX
Reflection

*Were entirely ready to have GOD remove all these defects
of character.*

Thirty-five days sober, and this time is different. I have taken the initiative to finally make a difference in my life. When I thought I was a done and ready to give up, I found that I still had one more pull left inside me. It's a struggle but I am pulling through, asking GOD to remove all my defects, and praying that I will get a second chance at life.

I look at what the last ten years have done to me. I have nothing to show for, not even a penny to my name. I have the education to get a good job but can't find any place that will hire me. The struggle is real. When will I get that chance to prove that my life has changed? My background is killing me, yet I am still here trying everything I can to succeed.

My illness of addiction has taken over my life and has been the ruler for the last ten years of my life. It's time to take a stand and fight for what I want. All I am asking for is a chance to prove that I am a good human being outside this character flaw that has haunted me for the last decade.

Society has trouble seeing through this mask that covers an addict. All they see is our defaults and character defects when substance use is present. In all honesty, as an addict, all I wanted to feel was normalcy and to be happy with life. I just wanted to fit in again and not feel judgement from every eye that looked at me. Substance made that feeling of judgement go away.

"Liquid Courage," "Truth Serum," or "Shot of Life" are the phrases used by many addicts, for it's what you feel emotionally when any substance runs through your body. My inhabitations were lowered, and the standards I once lived by were gone. Where is the quality of life when I find myself dealing, stealing, and doing just about anything to find my next high? That's what has taken over my life now.

Forget about the job. Forget about taking care of your child. Forget about helping with the chores around the house, the list will go on and on of all the things I forgot about when it came to my addiction if it interfered with my ability to get high.

I could not afford to pay for my drug of choice anymore, so I chose to deal it and found that was quick and convenient. I did not have to worry about money, nor did I ever have to worry about going dry for I had it always readily available. It's what I stooped to in my life. It was endless days of not sleeping and being emotionally numb to the world around me for all I could think about was Meth or that drug I used to feel normal again.

Feeling normal has its consequences. People would ask why you can't just get a job and forget the drugs that have you so convicted in life. First, once you got a criminal record, your professional background is pretty much over. I don't have the money to fight for what I once had, nor do I have the mental stability to take another blow to my ego when society tells me, "NO, you're not eligible."

I have the capability to be what I once was, but all the baggage and history I left behind during my drug use will haunt me for the rest of my life. It has left me no choice, application after application, in one year, I literally submitted 365 job applications. I had only one interview, and I was not hired for the position offered, even though I was qualified to do what was asked of me, but with my history and record, I was denied employment. All I am asking for is a chance to prove myself.

I believe if I was given a chance to prove myself, my life would have been different. I wouldn't have resorted back to the street life where I had to deal drugs to survive. Today, I asked GOD to remove all my character defects that I have learned over the last ten years, so my true self can shine again. Then my life will be whole again.

CHAPTER SEVEN
Humility

Humbly asked him to remove our shortcomings.

After everything I have been through, a person might say, "That is it; I am done; I give up." How can I continue life after everything? People would always say, "GOD will only give you what you can handle." How much more can I get and deal with before I am done? When will it be my turn to live life and enjoy it without pain and suffering?

I believe many addicts ask that question. It's the question why? Why blame GOD? We were all given the free will to make our choices and I do believe that we all have a purpose in life. Life is a precious thing to have. I have only one life to live. So, I take this time to reflect on what I have and what I have lost.

I have had the opportunity to become a father. There are many people who are not able to experience this. It was a wonderful gift that I was given, and I do enjoy being a father. Fatherhood is stressful but it's a wonderful job. I express it as a job for it is something that a person continues to learn and grow with. Fatherhood is a skill that over time and with experience has made me become a better person. I learned to open my heart and love others no matter what or who they are.

I've had the chance to experience a miracle when my son was alive. This child was a wonderful human being, and in his short time, he taught me how to be strong when times were rough. He taught me how to persevere.

As a child who was born with a muscle disease and lived a hard life with his challenges, Jonathan never went a day without smiling. Every picture I have of him, there was genuine smile of happiness. Jonathan was happy up until the day he died. GOD, I could not have asked for more than that.

Jonathan was loved by so many people. He was an old soul in a young man's body. He struggled everyday but he did not let that slow him down. I still remember the day when he became a big brother. He was so proud when he held little Haylee in his hands. Again, that smile appeared, and he said, "I am a big brother."

Jonathan's death not only showed the vulnerability of life, but he also showed me that no matter the situation, you can be happy. It took me a long time to get here and to be able to understand that. Grieving a loss of a child is the worst nightmare anyone can ever experience. Letting go of his memory and allowing him to be an angel was even harder. I could not hold on to this pain and anger anymore. It was always that question WHY?

I had to let this go and never ask the question of why anymore. GOD had a plan for Jonathan, and he was not able to live a full life here with us, but he will live an eternal life as an angel. I understand that I can't see him anymore but that doesn't stop me from thinking and talking to him. I have a place in my heart that will always carry his memory. I can't be angry at GOD for this anymore.

I humbled myself and learned that I can't be greedy anymore with life. GOD deserves little children in his kingdom just like we do. All I must do is open my heart to him and tell him what needs to be said, and that is what I do.

On every birthday he would have had, and any moment that I feel sorrow, I get a helium filled balloon and write all my messages to Jonathan on there. Then, I release it to the open air and watch it rise into the sky where it will finally disappear. Once it disappears, I know that Jonathan has received my message.

I learned from all of this is that I am human and no different than anyone else. We are bound to make mistakes and learn life lessons from those mistakes. I don't deserve to be better than that person next to me, for we don't know what that person has been through. Their story can be worse than mine and even more traumatic. I can only do what Jon-boy would do and extend my hand and help pick those who have fallen and show them the way to happiness.

CHAPTER EIGHT
Amends List

Made a list of all people we had harmed and became will-ing to make amends to them all.

Sitting in my own prison of life during my addiction not only hurt me but hurt many people I loved. There's not a soul on this earth that I would not give my last shirt to help. I have learned throughout my journey that I have had many co-dependencies that enabled me and fueled my addiction habits.

I would always put another person before helping myself. Of course, it makes me feel wonderful to help another, but what benefit do I get if I can't help myself? Sounds very selfish, you might say, but in my addiction, I learned that it's about me and no one else. I can only help myself and pull myself through this period. I must put myself first and concentrate on making my true self better.

What good am I if I don't help myself before I help another? If I continue with such behaviors, I am only signing my own death warrant, and if I am dead, how will I be able to help others? As part of my healing process, I made a list of people that were hurt by my addiction. With that list, I began to write each person to explain what happened to me and how my addiction affected my life. I would love to have their forgiveness, but I understand that not every person will forgive me for what I have done.

The only thing I can hope for is that they understand they are not at fault and give them more insight about how my addiction destroyed my life. It's about making amends to those whom I have hurt during my addictions. Reaching out to those individuals I have hurt not only shows I am accountable for my actions but also shows that I recognized the wrong that was done to them. I pray to GOD every night to forgive me for my wrong doings and to heal those who were wounded by my addiction. From here, I must move forward with life knowing I did everything I could to amend my relationships and accept whatever response I get from those who were hurt.

CHAPTER NINE
Made Amends

*Made direct amends to such people wherever possible,
except when to do so would injure them or others*

"To those who I have hurt in my past, I hope you can find it your heart to forgive me for my wrongdoings. My addiction took me to a place of darkness where I not only hurt myself, but I hurt you as well. It was not my intention to hurt those whom I love, and I live with this pain every day, knowing I hurt you, and I am truly sorry. Addiction is a horrible illness, and it has taken everything from me."

"I am working hard every minute of every day to remain sober and better my life. Hopefully, with this hard work, I will one day be able to enter your life again and show you that you have a place still in my heart. I understand that if I can't, I will have to accept that response and move forward. I am getting help now and receiving great insight on how to let go of my past that has haunted me. With this help, I have opened a new chapter of life where I will be my true self once again. I wish you the best and know that I will not allow my addiction to hurt another person."

CHAPTER TEN
Continued Inventory

Continued to take personal inventory and when we were wrong promptly admitted it.

Sobriety is a new part of my life that I must nourish just like a relationship. It's my relationship to myself, the one that is most important. Every day I wake up, I thank GOD for another day of sobriety and reminisce on all my good things that have happened since I had decided to be sober. Trust me, it's a job to maintain my sobriety for all the temptations I face each day. I don't remember who once told me this, but a habit is developed in less than thirty days but takes a lifetime to break.

Since I stopped using drugs and sought help from professional mental health advocates, my life has begun to turn around. Things are finally looking bright in my future once again. My head is no longer clouded by substance. My memory is improving significantly each day. Relationships that were once burdened by my addiction have begun to heal, and I have gained hope and started a new journey where I will remain sober.

Attending my meetings, group therapy, and individual therapy, using new coping skills, and always taking inventory of what I have in my life now is my everyday norm. Walking lightly and keeping my guard up since my demon will always be following me. No matter where I go, it will be right there on my tip toes. All it will take is one bad moment or tragedy and I could spiral out of control with a relapse.

It's my reality, and I must face and understand how sensitive the situation is and not test the waters. Addiction is an illness that will last a lifetime, and I hope and pray that a relapse will never happen again. A relapse will always be imminent in my future. It's not that I know it will happen. I just tell myself this for if it should ever happen, I am not held down with terrible depression and self-hate. I will promptly admit that I was wrong and seek help right away. That is the first step of my plan.

I will continue to work on new coping skills, taking note on the ones that work and disregarding the ones that don't. My sponsor will be on speed dial number one on all my phones, and if I ever feel that emotion of despair and/or the urge to use, my sponsor will be the first person I call. I will keep honest and good people around me that understand my illness and how vulnerable I am to drugs. This will keep me accountable for my actions and help direct me to a safe place where I can deal with situations that may challenge my sobriety.

With practice and help from my advocates, I have a better chance of not relapsing. I must stay on track and never let my guard down. I must also recognize and avoid situations that trigger my addiction. These are practices that I must do to stay sober. I have come too far to let myself go again to the dark side of my addiction. I will fight for my freedom and life because it's worth fighting for.

CHAPTER ELEVEN
Spiritual Growth

Sought through prayer and meditation to improve our conscious contact with GOD as we understood Him, praying only for knowledge of His will for us and the power to carry that out.

Throughout my journey of life and dealing with my illness, I have always had trouble trusting my faith in GOD. I always questioned him on why my life was so hard and why I have endured so many tragedies in my life. I was raised as a church-going boy and had a very strong belief in my Higher Power, but overtime with everything that has happened to me, I began to lose that faith. I do believe a lot of addicts lose their faith in their higher power in whatever cultural belief they may have.

The word why was always in every question I asked GOD. Why did this happen to me? Why did you take Jonathan from me? Why did you allow me to go on a destructive path? Why did you not answer my prayers? The list can go on and on.

GOD is my almighty, and I believed that he let me down. He should have been there when I was alone crying over my son's death when no one else was. He should have been there when I asked to help me when I needed my pain and suffering to end and for him to show me happiness again.

When I began my journey with addiction, I lost all hope and respect to my GOD. This is where I went wrong. Like I said before, I was delt this deck of cards and it's my choice on how I played them. I found out that if you don't play it right, your life will spiral out of control. Most people would just get back up and try again and play that deck of cards again, but with my addiction, I decided to just accept what was given to me and believe that there was no other way. Of course, that is where my illness of addiction took over. It became that ruler of my life and pushed my GOD right out of the way.

I learned that is where I went wrong. My GOD was always there. I just had to take the time and look at what he taught me. He taught me so many different experiences. He taught me how to love. He gave me the feeling of despair, so I know what it was like to lose something I cared so deeply for. I look at life different now for what GOD has shown me, and I can't be angry anymore at him. It's not GOD's fault that my life was so terrible for he knew that I was always strong enough to handle whatever came my way.

During this step in my recovery, I had to forgive myself for where I went wrong and lost my faith. It was never GOD's intention to make me suffer. It was my own prison I made for myself. It's where my addiction took me that made my life so terrible.

I realized that the problem was me asking the question why. There is no reason to ask that question, and I finally saw that GOD was there to help me experience what life really is. I am not the only one out there that has experienced the things I have endured during my lifetime. GOD's intention was to show me these experiences so I can one day help others and show them the way to happiness.

My faith in GOD is now stronger than ever. I have decided not to allow my addiction to control my life anymore and allow my GOD to show me the righteous path he has for me. I will no longer defy my GOD. I will embrace his presence in my life and thank him for every day I live on this earth. I will just let go of what the past has been and hope that tomorrow will be a better day.

Restoring the hope in my life is what I needed. Without GOD, there is no hope, but with GOD, there is always hope for a better tomorrow. Each step I take forward now is getting easier and brighter with GOD at my side. "Thank you, GOD, for what you have shown me, and I promise never to lose my faith in you for I know you will never give me something I can't handle."

CHAPTER TWELVE
Giving Back

Having had a spiritual awakening as the result of these steps, we tried to carry this message to alcoholics and to practice these principles in all our affairs.

I am finally in a good place in my sobriety. I have been able to work through these steps with the help of my advocates. I have gained such great inspiration to remain sober now and learn more about my true self. The ability to overcome such a debilitating illness is an accomplishment. It takes the notion to want to change to make a change in my life.

Being true to myself and GOD is the only way now. Remembering that with GOD, all things are possible in life. I am no longer afraid to see what the future has in store for me. I am embracing the fact that I can deal with situations that may not go my way. I will not dwell on the bad of a situation but will look at what I can learn from it and move forward with the chance to make my life better from the experience.

Life is too short to ponder in the past. My life will end up passing me by if I don't let go of the past and embrace the future.

I will not be missing all the wonderful moments GOD has intended for me to experience and learn from. It's a wonderful thing to have this burden of guilt and shame lifted off my shoulders now. The only thing I feel now is the hand of GOD on my shoulder.

With my experience and knowledge of addiction, it's time for me to extend my hand to help others who have fallen to the dark side of their addiction. I will help those to see the light of GOD on the other side of this darkness that has surrounded them by living by example and giving inspiration to those who believe their lives have been lost and have no hope. I am allowing people to see how I overcame this illness and my hard work to remain sober is something worth fighting for. The darkness has now been lifted to allow the bright light of GOD to shine in is a wonderful feeling to have. I believe now that I have the strength to carry on and face the world with a different attitude and the motivation to begin a new life, a new life being sober and not clouded by substance.

I have made a promise to myself. That promise is to take care of myself so when the time comes, I can help the person who enters my life who is seeking help and guidance. I can carry on the help that once was given to me by following these twelve steps I took during my recovery.

CONCLUSION

I hope that by reading this book you have a better understanding of what an addict battles with every day. I never wish this upon anyone for the outcome is never good if they don't seek treatment. I don't care if a person says they have it under control or not. Eventually, the damage will surface.

Unfortunately for me, it took years of substance abuse before my damage was noticeable. By then, it was too late to save what damage had been done. I will have to live with my damage for the rest of my life. The thing that is different is that I will not allow my past to haunt me. I will persevere. I want to make this promise to everyone who reads this book, and that promise is:

"I promise with every day of my life, I will try to make a difference to the world by showing those who suffer from addiction that sobriety can be done. We can beat this illness of addiction one day at a time and live a healthy, normal life again." Taking this action and leading by example, I want to educate those who don't understand what an addict goes through. Life is not easy, and there will always be ups and downs. The important part is how an addict copes and deals with it.

To the loved ones who are affected by someone's addiction, please understand that this is an illness and treatment is available. Don't go at it alone. Seek help from a professional and confront this illness with compassion for it won't be easy at first. With help and counseling, things will get better if your loved one wants to change.

To all the people who are suffering from addiction, I want to challenge you. I challenge you to get sober for one day. If you can get through one day, you can do another. Take it one day at a time and before you know it, time will pass, and your life will turn around. Things will get better and the dreams you once had will begin to evolve if you believe you can do it. Remember that GOD is always on your side and with His help, you can beat this addiction.